MW01106539

This notebook belongs to:

-----------------------------------

Date:

-----------------------------------

Thank you for using this Blank Lined Journal.

Please feel free to give a review on Amazon if you found this journal to be helpful.

If you have a feedback or comments, please contact us at

www.ascenddigital.io

Made in the USA
Monee, IL
14 September 2021

78029866R00068